Photo by Hawthorne Studio

Rainbow River
by Katie Pasquini Masopust, 54″ × 80″, 1994

Transparencies of colors weave through this vertical landscape in a rainbow color scheme. From the Hendricks Collection.

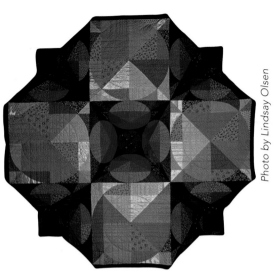

Photo by Lindsay Olsen

Melanie's Rose by Katie Pasquini Masopust, 72″ × 72″, 1982

This quilt is a study in transparency made to honor little Melanie Rose, who passed on at a very young age. The design is a mandala in a symmetrical radiating composition using a rainbow color scheme. From the collection of Randalyn Perkins.

Photo by Lindsay Olsen

The Juggler by Katie Pasquini Masopust, 80″ × 72″, 1985

A three-dimensional design, *The Juggler* uses a rainbow color scheme in a circular composition. Geometric forms create a fantasy place floating through space. The warm colors of the forms lead the eye around the platform. From the collection of Bob Masopust Sr.

Photo by Hawthorne Studio

Labyrinth by Katie Pasquini Masopust, 90″ × 85″, 1989

Labyrinth is made in a rainbow color scheme, using levels of cool and warm colors in an isometric grid composition. The visual layering is enhanced by color: the cool colors recede, with black receding the most; the warm colors come forward. From the collection of Bob Masopust Sr.

introduction

I LOVE taking painting classes. My paintings influence my quilts, and my quilts influence my paintings. It is a great give and take of ideas. Since 2002, I have been exploring different abstract design techniques. These techniques have developed into a two-day class on designing abstract quilts. I have guided students through these explorations, and many of their completed works are included here. In this book, I explain some of my ideas for creating unique art quilts and suggest different methods you can use to develop ideas on your own. You can work through the book by completing the explorations in the order that I have presented them, or you can start with the ones that look most exciting to you. It doesn't matter what order you do them in. Once you have a design, follow my instructions as I explain how to turn it into an art quilt.

I have found that there are five stages to making art quilts.

- Stage 1: Desire
- Stage 2: Design
- Stage 3: Pattern Preparation
- Stage 4: Construction
- Stage 5: Finishing

STAGE 1: DESIRE

The first stage is desire: the desire to express yourself creatively. There are many different media with which to create, but I am betting that if you are reading this book, your medium is fabric. Follow the five stages of quiltmaking, and you will be on your way to becoming a quilt artist. The desire stage is exciting and will get you thinking about what you want to create. The exploration chapters will explain how to design quilts using different game plans.

STAGE 2: DESIGN

The design stage begins with an initial inspiration, continues through making decisions about composition and color, and ends with analyzing your proposed design.

Inspirations

Design Inspiration

Inspiration, which comes in many forms, is needed to begin a design. I often use photographs as inspiration. I carry a camera with me everywhere and photograph flowers, landscapes, architecture, animals—anything and everything. Drawings or sketches can be inspirational. Great ideas can come from drawings and doodles, even if you think you can't draw. The act of drawing opens the right side of the brain and allows creative thoughts to come more readily. Painting is another wonderful way to find inspiration for quilts. Again, you don't have to be a great painter; a small section of a larger painting is all that is needed to create a dynamic art quilt.

This book contains ten exploration chapters with different design game plans to get your creative juices flowing. Read the chapters in any order you like, and if you get an idea that is different from what is presented in the instructions, go with it. The game plan rules are the restrictions I place on a design. If you don't have plans, then you have no direction. Creativity is making up exciting rules to follow for a particular design. These rules can change for each quilt.

Designs

Many students have told me that they find designing very stressful. Instead of thinking of design as hard, think of design as a game that you are playing. It is best to have rules to play the game. Use the left side of your brain to come up with the specific rules, then use the right side to design to those rules.

Color and Composition

Compositional layouts can help you organize the elements in a design. This organization is critical in allowing the viewer to understand the message of the design. There are many compositional possibilities to choose from.

A good color scheme can make or break a piece. You can choose from various classic color schemes—analogous, complementary, triad, and monochromatic are a few of these classic color schemes. Master painters have refined these color schemes over the centuries, and you can use them as guides. Additionally, remember that a full range of values, from light to dark, makes the difference between a mediocre quilt and a true piece of art.

Being Creative

I can create better when I pay attention to both the right and left sides of my brain. The left side is the analytical side, and the right side is the creative side. Both sides, of the brain are needed to create. Knowing when to use each side is helpful. The left side of the brain is used for deciding what rules to follow in creating the design and for determining how to construct the resulting design. The right side of the brain is used during the design stage.

There are ways to help the right side operate at its full potential. The right side of the brain does not like to be interrupted, talked at, or stressed out. Design time should be uninterrupted time. If I have a limited amount of time to design, I set an alarm clock so I won't be checking my watch constantly. Checking my watch is distracting and utilizes the left side of the brain. I also listen to right-brain music, such as classical, instrumental, or other music without lyrics to distract me.

Use the compositional layouts (page 12) and color schemes (page 14) included in this book as guides when designing your quilt.

Color wheel of seven-step value color cards

Analysis

It is important to analyze your designs before you start to work with fabric. This is the time to step back and observe with unbiased eyes. The Analysis chapter (page 20) contains questions for you to answer about your design. Your answers will help you evaluate the design's strengths and weaknesses. It is best to resolve any issues at the drawing stage rather than finding fault after the quilt is complete.

STAGE 3: PATTERN PREPARATION

After you have developed and analyzed a strong design, it is time to make the pattern. I use a template method that is easy and accurate. It allows you to use any shape, and all the pieces fit together perfectly. From Design to Pattern (pages 71–73) shows you all the steps.

STAGE 4: CONSTRUCTION

In the construction stage, you put together your quilt using the method that works best for your design. It is important to be as accurate as you can. This is when the left side of the brain is needed. Piecing and appliqué are the most popular ways to construct a quilt; both can be done by hand or machine. Fusing is a relatively new way of constructing a quilt, and I have even seen quilts made out of plastic or wood that are "sewn" together with staples or nails. Stretching outside your comfort zone can lead to beautiful and unique works. On pages 74–77, I explain how I construct my quilts.

Photo by Lindsay Olsen

Sampler by Katie Pasquini Masopust, 58" × 82", 1978

I made this quilt in the first quilting class I attended.

STAGE 5: FINISHING

This stage is about completing your piece. You can bind or satin stitch the edge, or sew it right sides together with a backing and turn it. Whatever method you choose, the finished edge should be appropriate for the overall quilt design and should be completed with care so it doesn't detract from the overall appearance. A hanging method, such as a sleeve, should be attached at this time. A label should be added that includes the title of the quilt, the name of the maker, and other pertinent information.

Always treat your finished art quilt with the respect it deserves. Document it with high-quality digital images. I recommend using a professional photographer. These images can serve a variety of functions: in show applications, presentations, and submissions for publication. Document any important information about the quilt's inspiration and construction. This will be helpful when writing an artist's statement or the captions for your work. Refer to pages 78–79 for finishing techniques.

Binding, sleeve, and label

Those are the five stages in the creation of an art quilt. I will explain each stage in greater detail in the following chapters. Let's get started!

tools and supplies

A FUN and important part of quiltmaking is the tools you get to use. Over the years I have tried hundreds of tools. The following includes the ones that work best for me.

CROPPING TOOLS

Cropping tools are used to cut down or block out parts of a design or painting that are not necessary to the composition. The best cropping tool is made from a precut mat used for framing pictures. Cut two opposite corners on the diagonal to create two L shapes. These L shapes can be opened and closed to create any size frame. This expandable frame can be placed over various areas of a photo or painting in the search to find the best part—the heart—to create a stronger composition. An empty slide mount can also be used as a cropping tool and is the right size for discovering fine details in inspiration photos or paintings.

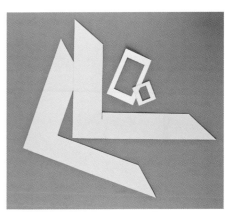

Cropping tools: precut picture-frame mat cut at opposite corners, empty slide mount, hole in card stock

PAPERS

Graphite Transfer Paper

Use graphite transfer paper to transfer drawings onto watercolor paper. It is like carbon paper but is made with graphite. You can find it at art supply stores.

Matte Acetate

The final designs are traced with a .01 Micron Pigma pen onto matte acetate. Matte acetate drawings enlarge cleanly to make a clear pattern for the templates.

Watercolor Paper

Use watercolor paper to test your color schemes and to create paintings for inspiration. It is important to use high-grade watercolor paper. Good-quality paper accepts the paint better. Low-grade paper will lose its tooth (the bumps in the paper) and will curl and get soggy. I use the 140-pound weight.

Tracing Paper

Tracing paper is perfect for trying out additions and corrections to a design.

Matte acetate, tracing paper, watercolor paper, graphite paper

PAINTS, BRUSHES, AND KNIVES

Watercolors

If you are new to watercolors, I recommend that you start with an inexpensive set; Prang is a good brand with strong colors. If you like this way of designing, upgrade to watercolors that come in tubes that you squeeze onto a palette.

Acrylic Paints

I recommend starting with inexpensive tubes or fluid acrylics that come in bottles. If you like painting with acrylics, upgrade to the more expensive tubes that contain stronger, more saturated colors. A diverse array of acrylic media are available; these are different liquids that you mix with the paint to change the way the paint is applied.

Brushes and Knives

Get the best brushes you can afford. A cheap brush will split, making funny marks and leaving hairs on your painting. I recommend the following sizes: 1″ flat, 3″ flat, and ½″ round. Other sizes are great, but these three are the bare minimum. Palette knives are for scooping up paint and spreading it on the surface. I use the 1″ triangle and the 3″ flat palette knives.

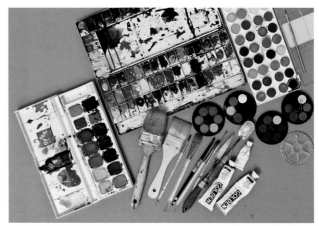

Inexpensive watercolor box, tubes, my paint box, acrylic tubes, cheap and good-quality brushes, and palette knives

FABRICS

Fused Fabrics

Fabrics and paper-backed fusible web are used for line explorations and can also be used in making mock-ups of your designs. For the exercises I use HeatnBond Lite fusible web.

Quilt Fabrics

Any fabrics can be used in making an art quilt. Assimilate into your stash some fine fabrics such as satins, Ultrasuedes, silks, and upholstery fabrics. Always use good-quality fabric so the piece will last for generations. I consider my fabrics my paints and like to have a wide assortment of colors, textures, and values available. I usually buy fabric in ⅓-yard lengths.

IMAGES FOR INSPIRATION

Photos, photos, photos. I use lots of photos and have a file of inspirational pictures. Get a good camera and learn how to use it. Taking pictures gets the creative juices flowing and can kick-start a design session.

MUSIC

I use different kinds of music for the different stages of quiltmaking. For the design stage, right-brain music is important—no words to distract, just pleasing rhythms that allow the right side of the brain to function. When all the creative decisions have been made, I switch to rock-and-roll music with a good beat to get me rolling along with the construction stage. Music, at whatever stage, should be enjoyable and nondistracting and should direct the energy in the room toward the task at hand.

Music CDs

Inspirational photos

Fabrics for art quilts

The first thing I do in a workshop is ask the students what their expectations are for the class. I often hear two major concerns. The first is, "I have all these ideas in my head, and I just can't get them out and onto the paper." The other is, "I can do these great designs, but I don't know how to realize them in fabric." In the exploration chapters that follow, I present guidelines to help you release those ideas from your head. In the construction chapters, I share my way of making the designs into quilts. By the time you reach the end of the book, you will feel confident in your ability to

- *Come up with an idea or design*
- *Draw the design as a well-thought-out composition*
- *Make the pattern*
- *Construct the quilt in the most functional way to create a completed work of art that you will be proud of*

composition

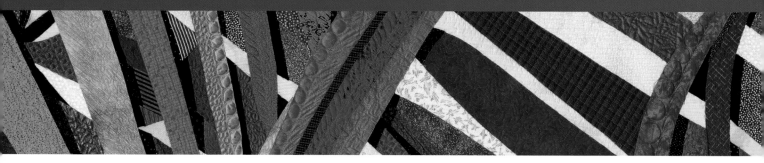

COMPOSITION IS the arrangement of the elements within a design. It is the most important part of the design process. Look to the inspiration photo or painting—all designs begin with the inspiration—to decide which compositional layout will work best. I consider the following six compositional elements when creating the game plan for my art quilts:

COMPOSITIONAL LAYOUTS

Compositional layouts are the classic ways to organize the elements in a design. This organization is critical in allowing the viewer to understand the message of the design.

For example:

Horizontal—calm
Vertical—growth
Diagonal—dynamic
Radiating—explosive
Circular—eternal
Triangular—uplifting
Framed—contained
Vanishing—depth
Grid—architectural
Overall—chaotic
Asymmetrical—off balance
Symmetrical—balanced

Horizontal Vertical Diagonal Radiating

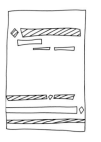

Circular Triangular Framed Vanishing

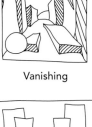

Grid Overall Asymmetrical Symmetrical

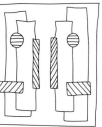

Compositional layouts

PATHWAYS

Pathways lead the viewer's eye through the piece. Pathways are created by lines, shapes, or colors that guide the eye to another set of lines, shapes, or colors.

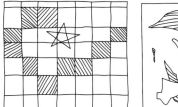  

Pathways

FOCAL POINTS

Focal points are created by contrast, and there are many ways to create them. The following are three that you can use when creating your art quilts.

- **Value contrast:** Using different values creates contrast. For example, placing the lightest fabric next to the darkest creates a contrast in value.

- **Color contrast:** Using different colors creates contrast. For example, a warm color provides contrast in a cool color scheme.

- **Shape contrast:** Using different shapes creates contrast. For example, you can create a focal point by adding a circle to a design of squares.

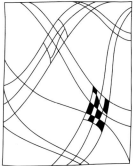  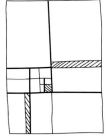

Value contrast   Color contrast   Shape contrast

Focal points

SPACE

Designs are made of negative and positive space. The negative space is the space around objects or shapes. Positive space consists of the objects themselves. The negative space needs to be as interesting as the positive space.

Good negative space   Bad negative space

Positive and negative spaces

SCALE

Scale is developed by using a variety of sizes of objects. Monotony occurs when everything is the same size. For example, areas that are small and busy should be balanced with larger, calmer areas that give the eye a place to rest.

Different scales

HARMONY

For a design to be successful, all of the above elements must work together in harmony, supporting the theme of the piece.

color

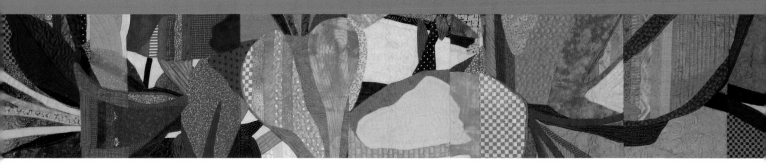

A S TEXTILE artists, we use fabric as our palette. I treat my fabrics as I would paints in a paint box. In my studio, they are arranged in the same order as the colors around the color wheel (shown on page 7). Not only do I have composition plans when I design my work, but I have color plans as well—they are the classic color schemes. They make for beautiful color choices. These are the ones I use most often.

COLOR SCHEMES

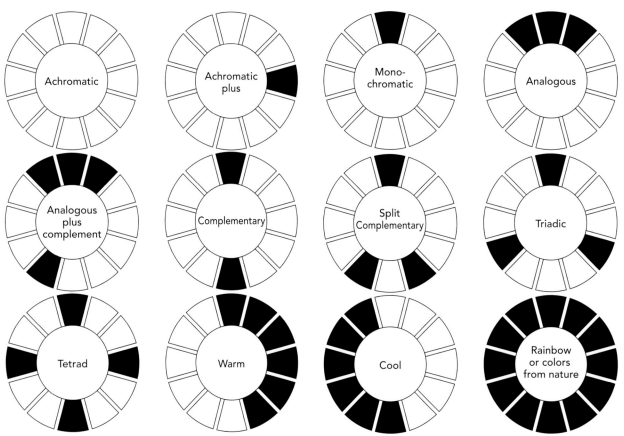

Classic color schemes

Achromatic

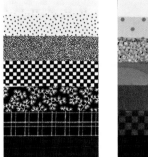

Achromatic is the absence of color. White, black, and all variations of gray make up the gray scale. A graphic gray scale can be created with black-and-white prints sorted to visually make a gray scale when seen from a distance.

Achromatic

Value 1: white-on-white prints

Value 2: white background with a little bit of black print

Value 3: white background with more black print

Value 4: the middle value, with equal amounts of black and white print

Value 5: black background with a lot of white print

Value 6: black background with a little bit of white print

Value 7: black-on-black prints

Monochromatic

Monochromatic is one color and all its values. This is an elegant color scheme and very calming. Contrast is created with value.

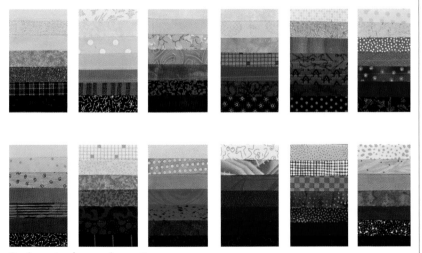

Twelve sets of monochromatic

Achromatic Plus

When assigning achromatic exercises to my students, I am often asked if it's okay to add a color—for example, black and white with a bit of red, or black and white with a bit of blue-green. For a true achromatic color scheme, no color should be used. But I have acquiesced on this point; it is more of a quilter's color scheme to use black and white with a bit of color for an accent. I call this scheme achromatic plus.

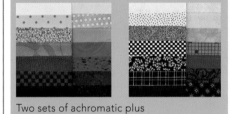

Two sets of achromatic plus

Analogous

Analogous colors are three to four colors next to each other on the color wheel. This is a harmonious color scheme; the colors are related because they are next to each other, and each color includes a bit of the neighboring color.

Three sets of analogous

Analogous Plus a Complement

The analogous plus a complement color scheme uses analogous colors plus the complement of one of the colors added as an accent.

Two sets of analogous plus complement

Complementary

The colors opposite each other on the color wheel are complements. These two colors create vibration and tension because they are opposites. When used in a medium value, these colors are very strong and demand attention, but when used with a full range of values, this color scheme can be quite pleasant. The addition of lights and darks creates a calmer composition.

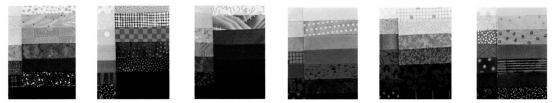

Six sets of complementaries

Split Complementary

A split complementary color scheme uses one color and the two colors on either side of that color's complement. This color scheme creates an effect that is similar to but softer than the complementary color scheme.

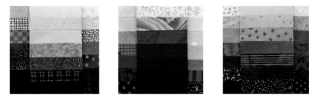

Three sets of split complementaries

Colors from Nature

This color scheme is used for realistic landscapes, creating the image in the true colors of the original subject.

Colors from nature

Triad

A triad color scheme uses three colors that are an equal distance from each other on the color wheel (i.e., separated by three colors). Red, yellow, and blue make up the primary triad color scheme. Orange, green, and violet make up the secondary triad color scheme. Two different triad color schemes are created from the tertiary colors (the colors between the primary and secondary colors).

 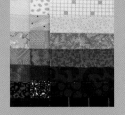  

Four sets of triads

Tetrad

A tetrad arrangement uses colors at four points on the color wheel, in either a rectangle or a square—in other words, two pairs of complementary colors. A dual complementary color scheme is a variation of a tetrad but uses two colors next to each other on the color wheel and their complements. This color scheme is very lively because of the use of two complements, but it can be toned down by using a full value run (covered later in this chapter).

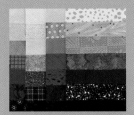  

Three sets of tetrads

Warm

Warm colors are yellow through red-violet, comprising one half of the color wheel. Warm colors are colors that are seen in fire.

Cool

Cool colors are yellow-green through violet—the other half of the color wheel. Cool colors are colors that are seen in water.

Rainbow

Rainbow colors are the twelve colors on the color wheel. This color scheme creates a rainbow effect. Warm colors come forward and cool colors recede when all the colors are used.

Warm

Cool

Rainbow

Three examples of full value range

VALUE

Value is as important as the colors you choose. It is often said that color gets all the credit while value does all the work.

I store my fabrics in racks of open bins in my design studio, separated into primary and secondary colors—yellow, orange, red, violet, blue, and green. I then sort each color further into seven value steps, from light (value 1) through the pure color to dark (value 7). Pure colors have an inherent value: yellow, yellow-green, and yellow-orange are value 3; violet and blue-violet are value 5; and the rest are value 4.

I use fabrics that read as one color. The fabric may include more than one color, but the overall impression is that of a single color. Busy fabric with too much pattern or color will compete with the lines of the design.

Using Value

I typically use three value ranges in my designs:

Full value range: A complete value range, or run, starts with the lightest value of a color, which is the color plus white (value 1), runs through the pure color, and ends with the darkest value, the color plus black (value 7).

Seven-step system for sorting fabric in wire drawers

Photo by Hawthorne Studio

Light value range: A light value range runs from the lightest value of a color (value 1) through to the midrange (value 3 to 5, depending on the color). It does not include the very darkest values of the color. This value scheme will create a light, cheerful quilt.

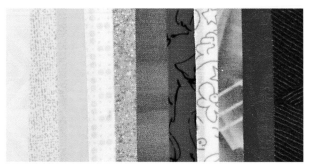

Light value range

Dark value range: A dark value range runs from the midrange value of the color (value 3 to 5, depending on the color) to the very darkest (value 7). It does not include the light end of the value run. This value scheme will create a somber or mysterious quilt.

Dark value range

Using the Seven-Step Value Range

I recommend that you try to arrange your fabrics into seven-step value ranges. Don't be too concerned with each piece being in the perfect order. If you can't decide if a piece goes in value 3 or 4, then it is close to where it should be and you can pick one or the other. Color and value will change depending on the lighting and the adjacent color choices. I use the seven steps as a guide, not as an absolute.

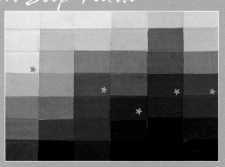

Pure color positioning

CHOOSING A COLOR SCHEME

When choosing a color scheme, begin by deciding on one color that you want to use. Find that color on the color wheel. Refer to the chart of color schemes and find all the other colors that would be needed for each scheme. You will know the right color scheme when you find the one that excites you. For the explorations based on painting, you will need to choose the color scheme before doing the painting. For the explorations based on drawing, this decision will be made after the design is complete. If you are working with a design based on a photograph, you will have additional information to help you in your decision making. For example, if the design is based on a flower or a landscape, decide whether you want to use colors from nature; if you do, create the design in the colors in the photograph. However, using an unexpected color scheme is one way of making a realistic design more abstract. For example, if the image is a red flower with green foliage, consider recreating it in a monochromatic color scheme using only purples, or possibly a triadic color scheme of red, blue, and yellow. An unusual color scheme will create a unique quilt that will catch people's attention and amaze them because the quilt is so different.

Along with color, the compositional elements of layout, pathways, focal points, space, scale, and harmony all contribute to the design and will play a part in making a truly artful quilt.

analysis

IT IS important to look at your designs and decide whether they have all the elements needed to make them harmonious. Analyze each completed design before you decide to make it into a quilt. Look over this list of questions, and respond with honest answers. The answers will help you find the strengths and the weaknesses of your designs and guide you in improving them.

QUESTIONS

- Is the composition (the arrangements of the elements), strong and clear?

- Does your eye move around the design, or does it get stuck in one spot?

- Are the negative spaces as interesting as the positive spaces?

- Are the design elements in a variety of sizes, or are they all the same size?

- Does the design need to be simplified?

- Would the design benefit from more detail in certain areas?

- Is there a dominant shape that is repeated throughout to provide unity, or is the design chaotic, with too many different shapes that don't relate to each other?

- Is there a focal point, or will the focal point be established through color choices?

- Are there clear visual pathways?

- Do you like this design enough to spend the time to make it?

Do the answers to any of these questions give you insight into what could be done to make the design stronger? If so, change the design now before proceeding further.

exploring SHAPES

G EOMETRIC SHAPES are the basis for many abstract designs. Two different geometric shapes are used as the basis of a design in this exploration. Some of the edges are erased to create overlaps, while other edges are echoed to create depth.

MATERIALS

Refer to pages 9–11 for tools and supplies.

- Pencil
- Compass
- Ruler
- Tracing paper
- Watercolor paper
- Graphite transfer paper
- Watercolor paints and small brushes
- Glue stick
- L-shaped cropping tool
- Matte acetate
- .01 Micron Pigma pen

INSTRUCTIONS

Start the Design

1. Choose a geometric shape—a square, rectangle, circle, oval, triangle, or other geometric shape.

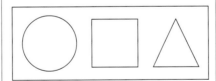

Choose geometric shape.

2. Draw 10 to 20 different sizes of your chosen shape on tracing paper. This shape will be the dominant shape in the design. Use a ruler or compass, or draw freehand for a more organic geometric shape.

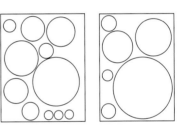

Draw multiple sizes of one shape on tracing paper or matte acetate.

3. Cut out the shapes, leaving a tiny bit of tracing paper outside the lines. This allows you to see the drawn edges when you are arranging the shapes. If you cut right on the lines, the shapes become invisible.

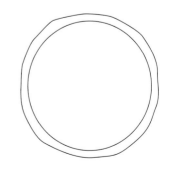

Cut out shape leaving margin.

4. Draw a frame around the edge of an 8½″ × 11″ piece of tracing paper. Place the tracing paper on a clean white surface so there are no lines underneath to distract you. Arrange the cut-out shapes within the frame. Glue the shapes in place. Look at the compositional layouts on page 12 to determine whether the placement suggests any of the compositions shown. See if you can move a few of the shapes to make the composition stronger.

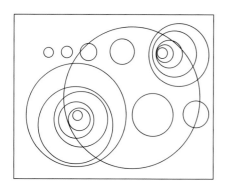

Arrange and glue shapes to paper.

5. Place another piece of tracing paper or matte acetate on top of this glued composition and trace all the shapes. This tracing will be the base of the design drawing.

6. Choose a second shape and draw 3 to 5 medium to large sizes on a piece of tracing paper. Cut out these shapes, leaving a bit of margin outside the lines.

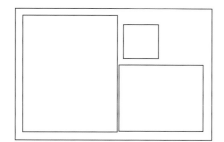

Draw another shape.

7. Add these secondary shapes to the original paper on which the first shapes are glued. Place them so that they work within the original composition, helping to unify the design and filling in some of the large negative spaces. Glue these shapes in place.

8. Place the tracing of the first shapes over all the glued shapes, and trace the secondary shapes.

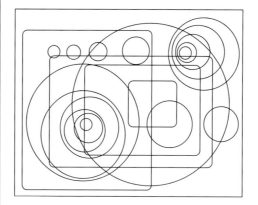

Glue secondary shapes, and trace.

The tracing may be complete at this point and ready to be used as the design for a quilt. Or, you can make the design more complex by erasing some lines and adding others.

Erase and Echo

Erase

Erasing some lines will create a layered effect. Determine which shapes you want to appear on top of other shapes. Erase the outline of the area where the shape underneath would be hidden. If there are places where many lines converge, erasing some of the lines often cleans up the design and gives more definition to the shapes. Some overlapping of shapes can be left in order to create transparencies, or the appearance of overlapping layers.

A combination of opaque and transparent shapes can be exciting.

Echo

Echo some of the shapes to create more interest and detail. Do this by drawing lines or curves that repeat the outline of the shape. Use different line widths and echo through different sections—in essence, weaving lines in and out of the elements that are already there.

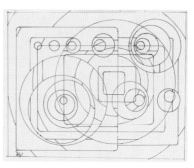

Erase lines and echo shapes to create more complex design.

Analyze the Design

1. Use the L-shaped cropping tool to see whether the design would be stronger if some of it were eliminated. Resize the frame created by the cropping tool, focusing on different sections to see whether the design is improved by cropping it tighter.

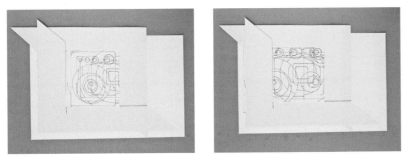

Two different possibilities with cropping

2. Analyze your design, using the questions on page 20. In this sample, I liked the entire drawing better than the cropped version.

Paint the Layout

1. Place the tracing paper design right side up on a piece of watercolor paper. Place a piece of graphite paper under the tracing paper design, and lightly transfer the image to the watercolor paper. Draw very lightly, so the transferred lines on the watercolor paper are barely visible; otherwise they may mix with the paint and create a muddy painting. Make 3 of these transfers to watercolor paper.

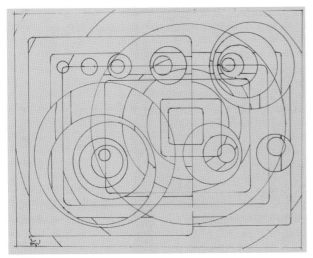

Make graphite transfers.

2. Choose 1 of the color schemes from pages 14–17, and fill in areas on 1 sheet of watercolor paper with paint.

Choosing Colors

When choosing colors, I find it helpful to choose one color or value within the color scheme and then paint the shapes that will help strengthen the original composition. Do this with a dominant color or value. Then choose another color or value. Paint those shapes that help support the first color or value placed in the composition. Then fill in the rest of the design with the other colors and values.

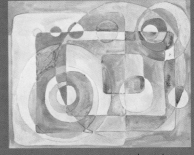

First painting uses warm color scheme.

3. Analyze the first painting. Often you find things that need to be changed or improved. A second painting lets you explore these options. Sometimes creating 3 or more paintings will help verify your design and result in a stronger piece.

Second painting uses more light; white paper was left to indicate very light values of chosen colors.

My students sometimes feel they don't know what they are doing and ask, "Where do I paint which color?" They worry about where each color should go and spend too much time in the left side of the brain trying to come up with all the right answers. The answer is that they are doing three paintings. The first should be just playing around with colors and values and their placement. Analyze the color placement to see what can be done to make the design better, and paint a second and possibly a third painting. Then, when all three paintings are complete, decide which one looks best. Ask yourself the questions in the Analysis chapter (page 20).

Finalize the Design

You are now ready to make the design into a pattern. Trace the final design on matte acetate with a .01 Micron Pigma pen. If you made any changes while painting—adding or eliminating lines or shapes—make those corrections on the acetate. Draw the design clearly and exactly how you want it to be for the pattern. Outline the design to make a frame.

Create the Quilt

Create the quilt by following the instructions on pages 71–79 for turning a design into a pattern, for construction, and for finishing.

Photo by Wendy McCerin

Warm Circles by Katie Pasquini Masopust, 42″ × 33″, 2005

In this quilt, I experimented by painting concentric circles, echoing the big circle on the right. I used a circular stamp to add little round dots and quilted around everything. The original layout of the circles created a horizontal composition, but with the addition of the squares and echoing circles, and the placement of the values, the composition changed from horizontal to circular. Notice how your eye moves around the quilt, bouncing from one light value to another through the different-sized circles.

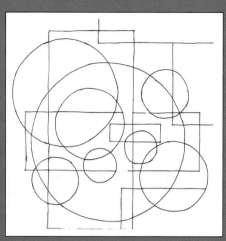

Two paintings for *Cool Squares* by Katie Pasquini Masopust

Exploration for *Bubble Wrap* by Judy Liebo

Exploration for *Oil on Water* by Cory Volkert

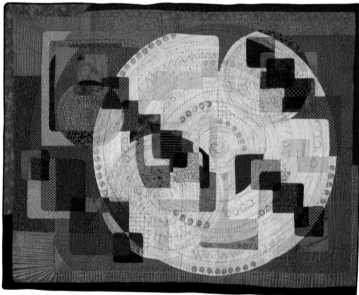

Cool Squares by Katie Pasquini Masopust, 42" × 33", 2005

As with *Warm Circles,* I added little dots with a round stamp. I used a felt pen and tube paint to create concentric circles around the big light circle. The large light circle creates a luminous backdrop for the darker diagonal, overlapping squares that float on the surface. The cool color scheme and diagonal composition make this quilt very different from *Warm Circles.*

Photo by Wendy McCerin

Bubble Wrap by Judy Liebo, West Linn, OR, 46" × 56", 2006

Oil on Water by Cory Volkert, Normandy Park, WA, 22⅝" × 32⅛", 2007

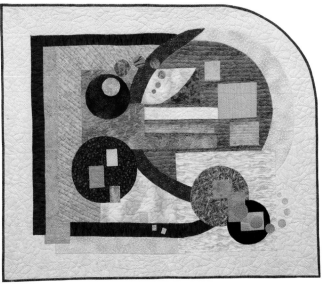

Galactic Metamorphosis by Deanna Ripley-Lotee, Ridgecrest, CA, 40¾" × 34", 2007

Circlesss I by Mary Vaneecke, Tucson, AZ, 41" × 29", 2007

Shapes in Space by Sandi Holland, Cortland, NY, 30" × 29", 2007
Quilted by Marion E. Lutz, Homer, NY

Exploration for *Circlesss I* by Mary Vaneecke

Exploration for *Galactic Metamorphosis* by Deanna Ripley-Lotee

Exploration for *Shapes in Space* by Sandi Holland

Exploration for *Shape Shifting*
by Brenda J. Stultz

Exploration for *Breaking Out* by
Terry Millett

Shape Shifting by Brenda J. Stultz, Fairmount, IL, 28½" × 36", 2007

Breaking Out by Terry Millett, Ridgecrest, CA, 32" × 42", 2007

exploring LINES

ARTISTS HAVE many
options when creating
designs with lines. Designs with
horizontal lines are peaceful and
can appear as landscapes; vertical
designs are uplifting and represent growth and new beginnings.
Diagonal lines are energetic and
dynamic. Lines that merge in the
distance create depth. Interwoven
lines create various kinds of grids.

Use different line weights or widths
to create variety. This quick exploration uses colored lines of fabric
fused to a 4" × 6" background.

MATERIALS

Refer to pages 9–11 for tools and
supplies.

- Paper-backed fusible web

- Fabrics in a chosen color scheme
  (You'll need small pieces approxi-
  mately 2" × 6", except for the
  background, which needs to be
  4" × 6".)

- Iron

- Rotary cutter, mat, and ruler

- Matte acetate

- .01 Micron Pigma Pen

INSTRUCTIONS

Create the Design

1. Pick a color scheme (pages
14–17), and choose fabrics that fit
into that scheme. Be sure to use all
7 values for each color, unless you
choose the rainbow color scheme.
For the rainbow scheme, use one
set of values (light, medium, or
dark)—using all the values of all the
colors would be too much for this
little exercise.

2. Iron the fabrics to a paper-
backed fusible web of your
choice.

3. Select 1 color for the
background and cut it into a
4" × 6" rectangle.

4. Cut the other fused fabrics
into thin strips—these are
the lines that will be used to
create the design. Decide on
a compositional layout from
page 12. Place the strips on
the background, arranging
them to reflect the chosen
compositional layout.

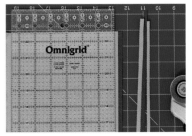

Cut thin lines from fused fabric.

Analyze the Design

Hang the piece on a wall, and study it. Can you do anything to strengthen the composition? If so, make another piece with the changes. Analyze both pieces by referring to the questions on page 20. Decide which piece is stronger—or make a third.

Three possibilities using complementary color scheme of violet/yellow in diagonal layout

Finalize the Design

You are now ready to make the design into a pattern. Pick the strongest composition and trace the design on matte acetate with a .01 Micron Pigma pen. Draw the design clearly and exactly how you want it to be for the pattern. Trace the outline of the piece to make the frame.

Create the Quilt

Create the quilt by following the instructions on pages 71–79 for turning a design into a pattern, for construction, and for finishing.

Exploration for *Rainbow Squared*: framed grid composition, medium-value rainbow color scheme, by Katie Pasquini Masopust

Rainbow Squared by Katie Pasquini Masopust, 33" × 42", 2004

This quilt uses colors to create distance. Yellow appears closest and violet appears the farthest away. This color theory guided me in my choice of colors. The front layer of yellow dots creates an implied line. The next layer is yellow-orange and orange lines, then the warm colors of red to red-violet, followed by the cool colors of green, green-blue, blue, blue-violet, and violet. This is a fun way to work with the rainbow color scheme. The background was pieced in black fabrics, Log Cabin style. Then the colored strips were turned-edge machine appliquéd on top to create the framed grid composition.

Photo by Wendy McCerin

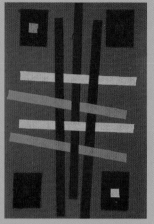

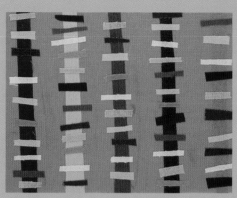

Exploration for *Irises*
by Greg Wilson

Exploration for *Houston Abstract 1*
by Maggie Farmer

Exploration for *Lines #3* by Sydne Bortel

Irises by Greg Wilson, Los Alamos, NM, 22″ × 34½″, 2007
Quilted by Nicole Dunn

Houston Abstract 1 by Maggie Farmer, Hereford, UK,
41½″ × 52″, 2007

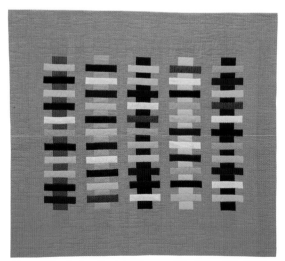

Lines #3 by Sydne Bortel, Tiburon, CA, 42″ × 37″, 2007

Happy Mistake by Kathy Roys Smith, Clayton, MI, 39" × 31", 2007

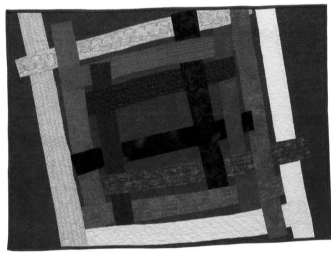

Gates by Barbara Shuff Feinstein, Stamford, CT, 40" × 29", 2007

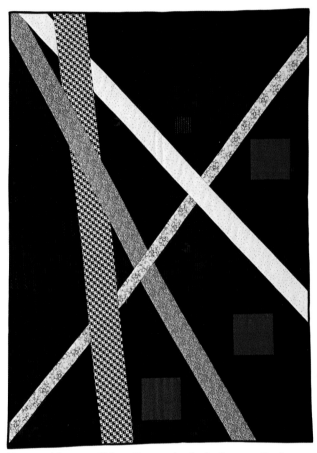

Lines and Squares: Ode to Suzanne by Becky Bostrom Strahan, Wilmette, IL, 36" × 50", 2007

Exploration for *Happy Mistake* by Kathy Roys Smith

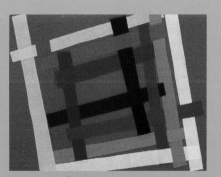

Exploration for *Gates* by Barbara Shuff Feinstein

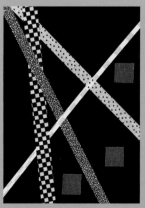

Exploration for *Lines and Squares: Ode to Suzanne* by Becky Bostrom Strahan

exploring DETAILS

INSPIRATIONAL PHOTOS come from everywhere. Great photos can come from a vacation or a trip to the market. Always carry your camera; you never know when a beautiful image will present itself.

Study the inspirational photo that you wish to use. Do you need to use the entire image to make a design? Often there is more in the image than you need to represent. The goal is to find a perfect little piece—the heart of the photgraph—that can be enlarged and enhanced to create a wonderful composition. An empty slide mount is the ideal cropping tool for this exercise.

MATERIALS

Refer to pages 9–11 for tools and supplies.

- Empty slide mount or $1\frac{3}{8}'' \times \frac{7}{8}''$ window in a piece of paper
- Inspirational photos
- Scissors
- Copy machine and copy paper
- Tracing paper
- Matte acetate
- .01 Micron Pigma pen

INSTRUCTIONS

Create the Design

Start with photographs that have interesting lines and shapes. Photos with close-ups of plants, animals, landscapes, buildings, or stones work well.

Start with photograph.

1. Use the empty slide mount as a viewfinder, and move it around the photographs, looking for an interesting composition. Refer to the compositional layouts on page 12 to help identify a good composition.

Use slide mount as viewfinder.

2. Slide matte acetate (matte side up) between the viewfinder and the photograph, and draw a line with the .01 Micron Pigma pen around the inside of the viewfinder. Remove the viewfinder.

3. Draw the shapes within the frame, still using the .01 Micron Pigma pen. Find 4 different little compositions—this could be 4 compositions out of 1 photograph, or 4 compositions from 4 different inspirational photographs.

Draw composition on matte acetate.

Creating Shapes

For this method of quiltmaking, all the elements must be drawn as complete shapes because the drawing will be enlarged for templates. A line must connect to other lines, or create closed shapes, to make the needed pattern templates.

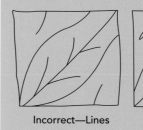

Incorrect—Lines   Correct—Shapes

Be sure to create closed shapes when drawing.

4. Cut the 4 little drawings close to the drawn frame.

5. Place the drawings side by side, 2 by 2, face down on the copy machine, and enlarge them by 400% to fit onto an 8½″ × 11″ piece of copy paper.

Prepare to enlarge 4 designs.

Analyze the Designs

Review your analyzed designs, choose the drawing that is most interesting, and clean it up by redrawing it onto matte acetate. Draw a frame around the drawing. Look closely at the photograph to see if there are other lines that can be added now that the drawing is bigger.

Redraw design on matte acetate.

Palms by Katie Pasquini Masopust, 51″ × 38″, 2004

I chose the achromatic-plus color scheme for this quilt about intense sunshine and the shadows it creates. From the collection of Randalyn Perkins.

Photo by Hawthorne Studio

Create the Quilt

Create the quilt by following the instructions on pages 71–79 for turning a design into a pattern, for construction, and for finishing.

Photo by Wendy McCerin

Weaving by Katie Pasquini Masopust, 50″ × 32″, 2004

I used an analogous color scheme of blue, blue-green, and green to create the weaving of the palm fronds. Dark shadows create greater depth between the three layers of this diagonal-grid composition.

Photo by Carolyn Wright

Double Weave by Katie Pasquini Masopust, 50″ × 32″, 2007

For this quilt, I chose the achromatic-plus color scheme to recreate *Weaving*. From the collection of Brian Harper.

Exploration for *Green Fantasy* by Martha Ainsworth

Inspiration for *The Wave I* by Nancy Evans

Inspiration and exploration for *Tree Study: Photo Section* by Phyllis Montgomery Tarrant

Green Fantasy by Martha Ainsworth, Sequatchie, TN, 20″ × 20″, 2007

Tree Study: Photo Section by Phyllis Montgomery Tarrant, Mint Hill, NC, 18″ × 27½″, 2007

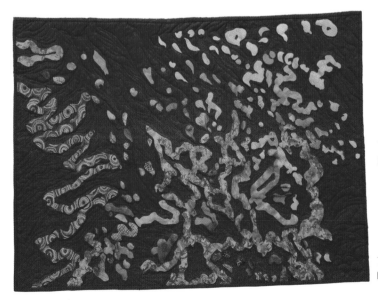

The Wave I by Nancy Evans, Catonsville, MD, 40½″ × 26″, 2007

Ernie by Belinda Heller, Antelope, CA, 53˝ × 53˝, 2007

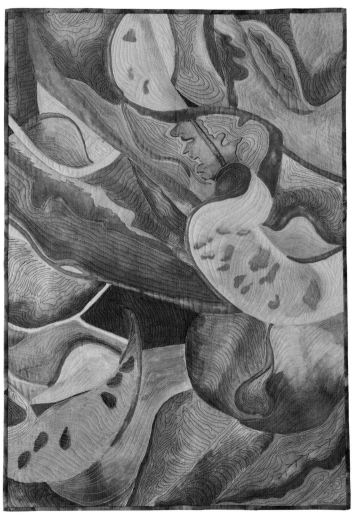

Abstract Flora by Ruth M. Bass, Springfield, OR, 29˝ × 39˝, 2007

Not All Lilies Are Tigers by Judy McKay, Chula Vista, CA, 25˝ × 37˝, 2007. Quilted by Carolyn Reynolds

Inspiration for *Ernie* by Belinda Heller

Inspiration for *Not All Lilies Are Tigers* by Judy McKay

Photo by Katie Pasquini Masopust

Inspiration for *Abstract Flora* by Ruth M. Bass

ADDING LINES

Adding lines can make your design more complex and abstract.

1. Start a design as described on pages 32–33.

Heart of photo in slide mount

Drawing of rose

2. Decide how to strengthen the design by checking the compositional layouts (page 12) for ideas. Place a piece of tracing paper over the acetate drawing. Try several different possibilities by moving the tracing paper and then using a different set of lines over the same drawing. One approach is to add lines that weave in and out of the elements by drawing through a shape, skipping the next shape, then

drawing through the next, and so on. Weaving lines through the design unifies all the elements and blurs the boundaries of reality to create a more abstract design.

3. Try at least 4 different possibilities by moving the tracing paper and adding different sets of lines.

Two possibilities for additional lines

Analyze the Designs

Cut out the different compositions you have drawn and put them on the wall to be analyzed. What if you don't like any of them? Draw more until you do.

Finalize the Design

You are now ready to make the design into a pattern. Trace the added lines onto the acetate drawing.

Photo by Carolyn Wright

Imagine by Katie Pasquini Masopust, 43″ × 67″, 2005.

I created *Imagine* using an analogous color scheme of yellow, yellow-green, and green. The light areas dance through the vertical strips in random movements across the top half of the piece, emphasizing the vertical composition. When my family was looking at the completed piece, everyone saw different things, imagining it to be something very different from the original rose.

Create the Quilt

When you have finalized your design, transform it into an art quilt by following the instructions on pages 71–79 for turning a design into a pattern, for construction, and for finishing.

Rainbow Lilies was inspired by photos of daylilies. The first and second photos lack interest, but the third has greater balance because it includes the bricks and the sidewalk. The composition flows diagonally from left to right, with the cracks of the sidewalk emphasizing the composition.

Drawing for *Rainbow Lilies* with addition of vertical lines to create feeling of growth

Photo by Carolyn Wright

First photo

Second photo

Rainbow Lilies by Katie Pasquini Masopust, 54″ × 37″, 2007. From the Hendricks collection.

I decided to make *Rainbow Lilies* using the rainbow color scheme in the full value range. Complementary colors used within each of the strips balance the colors as they move across the surface while enhancing the diagonal composition.

Third photo

Exploration for *A-peeling* by Judy Steward

A-peeling by Judy Steward, Hewitt, TX, 41″ × 33″, 2007

Acadia Summer by Susan Grancio, Reisterstown, MD, 42″ × 27″, 2007

Face Off by Carol Pope, Kerrville, TX, 25″ × 37″, 2007

Canopy by Robyn Moriarty Kruppa, Draper, UT, 23″ × 34½″, 2007

Inspiration for *Acadia Summer* by Susan Grancio

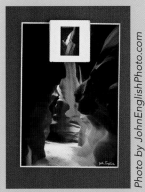

Exploration for *Face Off* by Carol Pope

Photo by JohnEnglishPhoto.com

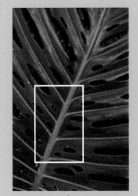

Inspiration for *Canopy* by Robyn Moriarty Kruppa

exploring REPETITION

REPETITION CREATES movement and emphasis. In this exploration, an image is repeated in different sections called cubes. The center cube contains the complete image. Each cube that is added contains portions of the image. Use different sizes of cubes to create more depth.

MATERIALS

Refer to pages 9–11 for tools and supplies.

- Inspirational photograph or image
- Ruler
- L-shaped cropping tool
- Copy machine
- Matte acetate
- .01 Micron Pigma pen

INSTRUCTIONS

Create the Design

1. Choose a photograph that has distinct lines and shapes. Use the L-shaped cropping tool to determine whether the entire photograph or image is needed. For this design technique, it is important to have interesting elements in the corners because the corners are repeated most often.

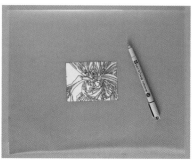
Consider photos to use.

2. Place a piece of matte acetate over the photograph. Use the .01 Micron Pigma pen to draw everything in the selected viewing area as enclosed shapes (page 33). Draw the value changes within the objects as well as the objects themselves.

Make line drawing using enclosed shapes.

3. Trace the design in the middle of a large piece of matte acetate.

Trace design in middle of acetate.

4. Enlarge the original drawing by 125% and 150% to give yourself 2 different sizes from which to choose.

Make two sizes of one drawing.

5. On the large piece of acetate, add a portion of a second cube tucked next to the original cube. Draw a portion of the original image, or an enlarged copy, within this new cube.

6. Move around the center, adding
portions of cubes. Draw the image
within the new cubes until the
design is complete.

Place 4 portions of design around center
cube.

Analyze the Designs

Create several design possibilities,
and hang them on the wall. Analyze
them for composition and interest
by answering the questions on
page 20.

Finalize the Design

You are now ready to make the
design into a pattern. Pick the
strongest composition and if
needed trace the design on matte
acetate with a .01 Micron Pigma
pen. Draw the design clearly and
exactly how you want it to be for
the pattern. Trace the outline of the
piece to make a frame.

Create the Quilt

Create the quilt by following the instructions on pages 71–79 for
turning a design into a pattern, for construction, and for finishing.

Photo by Carolyn Wright

Color Explosion by Katie Pasquini Masopust, 80″ × 60″, 2005
From the Hendricks collection.

The inspirational photo for this quilt was monochromatic green. I wanted to get as
far away from that green as I could to emphasize the lines of the leaves and make it
more abstract, so I chose to use the rainbow color scheme in a radiating composition. I used light values of the colors and white-on-white background fabrics in the
center cube; as the cubes move out from the center, the colors become darker in
value, and the background fabric becomes darker as well, as black-and-white prints
replace white-on-white fabric.

Sedona Cactus photos in two sizes

Sedona Cactus drawing

REARRANGING PIECES OF THE IMAGE

Another way to create repeat designs from one image is to make several photocopies of the original image, cut them into squares or rectangles, and arrange them to create the design. That is how I designed *Windmills.*

1. Choose a photograph and create a line drawing on acetate with a .01 Micron Pigma pen.

2. Make multiple copies of the line drawing on a copy machine. Arrange the copies or portions of the copies into cubed sections to create the desired composition.

Photo of windmill

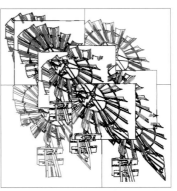

Arrange copies using left and right sections.

Photo by Hawthorne Studio

Sedona Cactus by Katie Pasquini Masopust, 50″ × 80″, 2004

I created *Sedona Cactus* in the colors-from-nature color scheme, emphasizing the red and green complementary colors. It was the first cubed piece that I made. I added small cubed sections all around the central cactus. I like the way the buds of the cactus repeat in a diagonal direction to emphasize the diagonal composition. From the Hendricks collection.

Photo by Hawthorne Studio

Windmills by Katie Pasquini Masopust, 60″ × 60″, 2004

I chose a warm color scheme to make the windmills stand out from the cool gray background. I used little bits of Ultrasuede to create the hardware on the windmills. Ultrasuede is good for small pieces because it will not fray, so you don't have to turn the edges. The repeated images form a diagonal composition. From the Cargill collection.

Zooming In

For Casablanca Lilies, *I started by taking pictures of a vase of lilies. I cropped the image with my cropping tool but didn't like the chaotic look. I then took just two lilies and photographed them by zooming in. I didn't need a whole bouquet to show the beauty of the individual blooms.*

Photos by Katie Pasquini Masopust

Three sizes of Casablanca lilies layered to create composition

Photo by Hawthorne Studio

Casablanca Lilies by Katie Pasquini Masopust, 54″ × 54″, 2005

I used colors from nature to create this quilt; I love the high contrast between the white of the flowers and the deep green leaves. The repeating images form a radiating composition. From the Hendricks collection.

Photo by Hawthorne Studio

Steps by Katie Pasquini Masopust, 47″ × 50″, 2000

I merged two sizes of circular brick steps to create this repetition in a radiating composition. I used the analogous plus a complement color scheme, with the transparent green leaves symbolizing how nature takes back what man has built.
From the Robertson collection.

COMBINING IMAGES

Another option is to combine multiple images in one design.

Draw the different images on acetate with a .01 Micron Pigma pen. Decide how you want them to go together, and draw them on a full sheet of acetate to create the design. Consider the different sizes you can use to create variety.

Photos by Katie Pasquini Masopust

Lotus bud and flower

Photo by Carolyn Wright

Lotus by Katie Pasquini Masopust, 60˝ × 60˝, 2005

I created *Lotus* in the complementary color scheme of red-violet and yellow-green. I used two different stages of the lotus plant's life; the open flower is a large size that covers the entire quilt. I added three cubes to place the same flower in a smaller size. A rectangular cube was added in the center to superimpose the beginning of the lotus life as the bud. Opportunities to use transparency were created where shapes overlapped within the cubes. These transparencies help unify this radiating design. From the Hendricks collection.

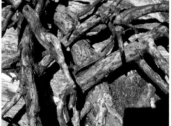

Inspiration for *Fractures* by Marianne Bender-Chevalley Villeneuve

Fractures by Marianne Bender-Chevalley Villeneuve, Switzerland, 48˝ × 36˝, 2006

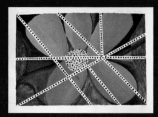

Inspiration for *A Day at the Beach*
by Mary Manahan

Inspiration for *Mother Nature's Helper*
by Brigitte Knobel

Exploration for *Bird's Eye View*
by Jennifer Conrad

Bird's Eye View by Jennifer Conrad, Owings Mills, MD, 37″ × 33″, 2007

Mother Nature's Helper by Brigitte Knobel, Kandergrund,
Switzerland, 43″ × 34″, 2006

A Day at the Beach by Mary Manahan, Newtown, PA, 50″ × 37″, 2007

Forest Hills Iris by Susan Vassallo, Gilbert, AZ, 50″ × 72″, 2007

Logs by Brenda H. Smith, Flagstaff, AZ, 41″ × 65″, 2007

Summer Succulents by Suzanne Michelle Hyland, Cottonwood Heights, UT, 34″ × 34″, 2007

Inspiration for *Logs* by Brenda H. Smith

Exploration for *Forest Hills Iris* by Susan Vassallo

Inspiration for *Summer Succulents* by Suzanne Michelle Hyland

Photo by Saroja Palagiri

Inspiration for *Toucan-N-Around*
by Jacquelyn Fox

Inspiration for *Organic Fantasy*
by Kay Young

Inspiration for *Saroja's
Dahlia* by Mary K. Reed

Inspiration for *Roussillon
Cubed* by Diane Ansel

Toucan-N-Around by Jacquelyn Fox, Greenwood, IN,
29˝ × 30˝, 2007

Saroja's Dahlia by Mary K. Reed, Jonesboro, IL, 40˝ × 32˝, 2007

Organic Fantasy by Kay Young, Shelby, NC, 52˝ × 36˝, 2007

Roussillon Cubed by Diane Ansel, Mill Valley, CA,
34˝ × 41˝, 2007

exploring
BLIND PAINTING

I **OFTEN** hear my students say, "I can't paint!" This exploration will place you on the path to painting. It is a nonthreatening first step. You don't have to be responsible for your painting because you will be painting blindfolded. So, no stress! Use acrylic paints with a large brush. Let music guide you—move the brush to the rhythm. When the paint is dry, move the L-shaped cropping tool across the painting to find the heart of the image in the explosion of color and movement.

MATERIALS

Refer to pages 9–11 for tools and supplies.

- Roll of white paper to cover a 6′ table twice (available at craft stores)
- Acrylic paint in chosen color scheme
- Paper plate for palette
- Large paintbrush 3″ or larger
- Blindfold
- 6 different types of music
- Friend to play music
- Paint smock or shirt
- L-shaped cropping tool
- Matte acetate
- .01 Micron Pigma pen

INSTRUCTIONS

Create the Painting

1. Cover a 6′ table with 2 layers of white paper.

2. Put on a paint smock, and have a blindfold handy.

3. Pick a color scheme, and place large amounts of each color on a paper-plate palette.

4. Chose 6 different pieces of music from different genres, and have someone help you by playing a selection of each type of music for you while you paint.

Music that I like includes the following:

> Rock-and-roll
>
> New age
>
> Classical
>
> Reggae
>
> Blues
>
> Jazz
>
> Country

5. Put on the blindfold, and pick up the paper plate and paintbrush. Have your helper play the first piece of music. Think about different types of paint strokes that go with the music, such as a rolling movement, swirling, short strokes, long strokes, dabs, and so on. Practice these in the air for a few minutes as the music begins; be sure to use your whole arm.

Paint for 30 seconds to a minute. Stop and move over one step, and prepare to paint again. Have your helper play the second piece of music. This time paint with a different type of stroke. Step once more to a clean place, and paint with a different stroke to the third piece of music.

Blind painting

6. Remove your blindfold, and analyze your paper. Do you have more paint on the paper than you thought, or much less? Are all the strokes similar? If so, what can you do differently to add more variety to the strokes?

Three different renditions of music on paper

7. Repeat the exercise with the second length of paper while listening to the remaining 3 pieces of music. If you had too little paint the first time, dip your brush into the palette more often. If you had too much paint, paint until you feel your brush becoming dry.

8. Let the paintings dry overnight.

Create the Design

1. Use the L-shaped cropping tool to search for the perfect spot, the heart of the painting. Refer to the list of possible compositions on page 12 to help you discover the jewel-like qualities of these paintings.

Using the Cropping Tool

I find that I am most successful in finding good compositions when I keep the L-shaped cropping tool open only 3"–6".

2. Draw around the frame created by the cropping tool. Cut the little paintings on the drawn line, and place them on the wall to be analyzed. Look for a strong composition. Pick the one you like best.

2½" × 5" cropped image from large blind painting in triadic color scheme of red, yellow, and blue

3. Lay a piece of matte acetate over the little painting, and with a .01 Micron Pigma pen draw all the shapes. Each shape must be enclosed. Look carefully, and draw around color changes as well as the small dots that are created by a dry brushstroke.

Line drawing of blind painting, used for *Paint* (next page)

Analyze the Design

Analyze your design, using the questions on page 20.

Finalize the Design

You are now ready to make the design into a pattern. If you need to correct the design, redraw the final design on matte acetate with a .01 Micron Pigma pen. Draw the design clearly and exactly how you want it to be for the pattern. Trace the outline of the piece to make a frame.

Create the Quilt

Create the quilt by following the instructions on pages 71–79 for turning a design into a pattern, for construction, and for finishing.

Exploration for *The Arch* by Ellie Sigler

The Arch by Ellie Sigler, Paris, France, 33½″ × 33½″, 2005

Photo by Wendy McCerin

Paint by Katie Pasquini Masopust, 60″ × 45″, 2004

I used white bridal satin to represent the white of the paper and used a triadic color scheme for the paint. Bridal satin is crisp and shows off the machine quilting beautifully in this diagonal composition.

Photo by Carolyn Wright

Fortissimo by Katie Pasquini Masopust, 79″ × 70″, 2006

I made this quilt in the analogous color scheme of blue, blue-violet, violet, and red-violet using a circular composition. *Fortissimo* is a musical term meaning very loud. From the collection of the Nebraska Quilt Study Museum.

4th of July by Sandra E. Lauterbach, Los Angeles, CA, 18″ × 21″, 2007

Photo by Carolyn Wright

Leggero by Katie Pasquini Masopust, 78″ × 81″ 2006

I like using the triad color scheme, and I again used it on bridal satin for this radiating composition. *Leggero* is a musical term meaning light and airy.

Exploration for *Leggero* by Katie Pasquini Masopust

Exploration for *Fortissimo* by Katie Pasquini Masopust

Exploration for *4th of July* by Sandra E. Lauterbach

Exploration for *The Wave*
by Sue Wilson

Exploration for *Molten* by Jeanne Oberrieth

Exploration for *Tsunami*
by B. Anne Greene

The Wave by Sue Wilson,
Flagstaff, AZ, 19¼″ × 26¾″, 2007

Tsunami by B. Anne Greene,
Glenwood Springs, CO, 27″ × 36″, 2007

Molten by Jeanne Oberrieth, Pleasant
Valley, NY, 41″ × 27″, 2007

Dancing Solo by Cheryl Razmus, Crown Point, IN, 25″ × 38″, 2007

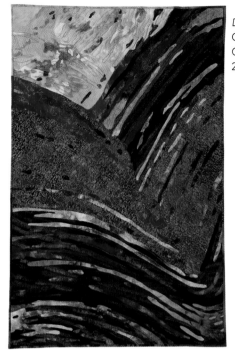

Celebration by Sandra E. Lauterbach, Los Angeles, CA, 18½″ × 28½″, 2007

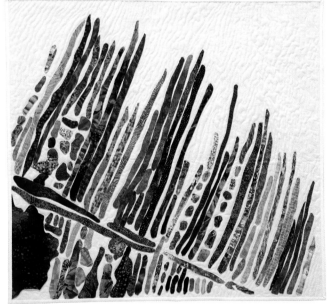

Brushstroke by Deanna Ripley-Lotee, Ridgecrest, CA, 28¾″ × 26¼″, 2007

Exploration for *Celebration* by Sandra E. Lauterbach

Exploration for *Dancing Solo* by Cheryl Razmus

Exploration for *Brushstroke* by Deanna Ripley-Lotee

exploring WATERCOLOR PAINTING

USING WATERCOLORS is a fun way to create abstract designs. Fill a large sheet of watercolor paper with controlled strokes, following your own game plan. Search the painting with the cropping tool to find the heart of the image to make into a quilt, or cut the whole sheet into squares or rectangles and reassemble them to create a different kind of design.

MATERIALS

Refer to pages 9–11 for tools and supplies.

- 18″ × 24″ piece of watercolor paper
- 2″ or larger foam brush or sponge
- Several different sizes of watercolor brushes (for example: ½″ round, 1″ and 3″ flat)
- Watercolor paint set
- Container for water
- L-shaped cropping tool
- Rotary cutter, ruler, and mat
- Matte acetate
- .01 Micron Pigma pen

INSTRUCTIONS

Create the Painting

1. Choose a color scheme from pages 14–17. If you are using watercolors in tubes, squeeze a bit of each chosen color onto a palette or paper plate. If you are using cake watercolors (these are hard watercolors in little tubs or rounds, like those we used as children, but also available in artist grade), wake up the colors by putting water onto each of the cakes that you will use; this softens them a bit so that you are able to get color onto the brush.

2. Use a foam brush or a sponge to slightly dampen the watercolor paper; this will allow the paint to move and blend when you brush it on. A completely dry paper produces a very sharp, hard line. Experiment with the amount of water needed, from dry paper to a very wet surface. The dampness changes the painting. This is the charm of watercolors.

3. Use brushes of various sizes to cover the surface with paint. Let the strokes cross each other and blend into each other. Have a plan in mind to make each painting unique. For example, use only vertical lines, or only curved lines, or a grid, or circles, and so on. (If all these ideas are used in one painting, it will become too chaotic—choose one idea and try to stick with it.) Use the different sizes of brushes to create a variety of marks.

Analogous color scheme of blue, blue-green, green, and yellow-green in grid layout

Triad color scheme of red, yellow, and blue in curved layout

Create the Design

1. When the painting is dry, use the cropping tool to search the surface for the heart of the image.

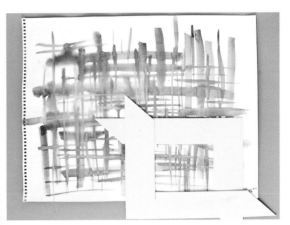

Crop on grid.

Crop on diagonal curve.

2. Use a .01 Micron Pigma pen to draw around all the shapes on matte acetate of the small section you have chosen. Be sure to draw the subtle lines created when the colors bleed together, and outline the section to form a frame.

Make line drawing on acetate.

Make line drawing on acetate.

Analyze the Design

Analyze your design, using the questions on page 20.

Create the Quilt

Transform your composition into an art quilt by following the instructions on pages 71–79 for turning a design into a pattern, for construction, and for finishing.

Teneramente by Katie Pasquini Masopust, 45″ × 60″, 2006

I used the triad color scheme of red, yellow, and blue for this diagonal composition. *Teneramente* is a musical term meaning with tender emotions. From the collection of the American Quilters Society Museum.

Syncopation by Katie Pasquini Masopust, 56″ × 40″, 2006

I chose a light-value analogous color scheme of yellow-green, green, and blue-green for this grid composition. *Syncopation* is the musical term for accented notes that fall on the weak beat. This grid composition reminds me of reflections in a puddle dotted with raindrops. From the Hendricks collection.

Exploration for *Marsh Morning I* and *Marsh Morning II with Red Sun* by Connie Smyer

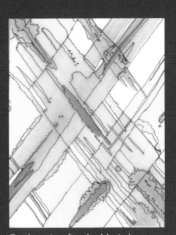

Exploration for *Au Matin* by Patricia Bliss

Exploration for *Deep Within* by Barbara Bowman

Marsh Morning II with Red Sun by Connie Smyer, Chandler, AZ, 14³/₈" × 16⁷/₈", 2007

Marsh Morning I or *Swirling Dawn* by Connie Smyer, Chandler, AZ, 14³/₈" × 16⁷/₈", 2007

Deep Within by Barbara Bowman, Clarksville, TN, 23½" × 38", 2007

Au Matin by Patricia Bliss, Glendale, AZ, 27" × 35½", 2007

RECONSTRUCTED SQUARES

Another way to use your watercolor paintings is to cut them into squares and reconstruct or rearrange the squares. The best paintings for reconstruction have marks of various sizes and areas that are different. An even, allover pattern will look the same when cut up and rearranged.

Grazioso by Katie Pasquini Masopust, 64" × 64", 2006

For this grid composition I used many values of the complementary colors red and green to recreate the bleeding of the watercolors in the inspiration painting. *Grazioso* is a musical term meaning gracefully.

Autumn Winds by Julie Banfield, El Sobrante, CA, 60¼" × 29½", 2007

Watercolor painting cut into 4" squares and reassembled for *Grazioso* by Katie Pasquini Masopust

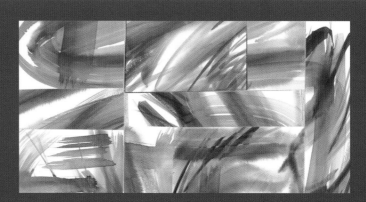

Exploration for *Autumn Winds* by Julie Banfield

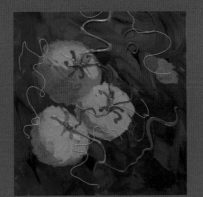

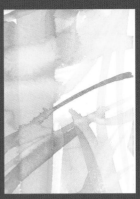

Exploration for *Transitions Are Messy*
by Priscilla Smith
Painting by Fran Early

Exploration for *Douglas, You Are One Hot Tomato!* by Karen Abramson

Exploration for *Wide Open*
by Marcia Bowker

Transitions Are Messy by Priscilla Smith, Chatham, MA,
63" × 63", 2006

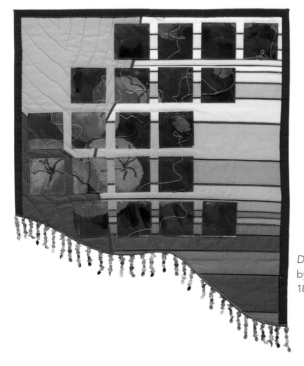

Wide Open by Marcia Bowker, Duluth, MN,
31½" × 41", 2007

Douglas, You Are One Hot Tomato!
by Karen Abramson, Poughkeepsie, NY,
18" × 16" 2006

exploring WATERCOLOR VIGNETTES

VIGNETTES ARE small explorations of colors and how they blend. When you paint six vignettes on a large sheet of watercolor paper, you will see how different types of strokes create different types of movement and emotion. These little paintings can be cropped again or used as a whole, floating on white.

MATERIALS

Refer to pages 9–11 for tools and supplies.

- 18″ × 24″ piece of watercolor paper
- Watercolor paints
- ½″ flat paintbrush
- Water
- Matte acetate
- .01 Micron Pigma pen

INSTRUCTIONS

Create the Painting

1. Visually divide the watercolor paper into 6 sections.

2. Choose a color scheme from pages 14–17, and prepare your paint by either adding water to the watercolor cakes or squeezing out a small amount of watercolor paint from the tubes onto a palette as described in Step 1 on page 54.

3. Load up the brush with 1 color, and make a different type of stroke in each of the 6 sections, using the edge of the brush as well as the wide part to create a variety of marks. Clean the brush, load it up with the second color, and make a second set of lines in each of the 6 sections. Repeat for all the colors in the color scheme. Fill the 6 sections of the paper with simple brushstrokes. Make the 6 vignettes as different from each other as possible so there will be a variety of designs to choose from.

Six small watercolor paintings

Analyze the Designs

By answering the questions on page 20, analyze the six designs to see if one has potential to be made into a quilt.

Create the Quilt

Pick the strongest composition and draw the design on matte acetate. Draw an outline of the design as a frame. Transform the design into an art quilt by following the instructions on pages 71–79 for turning a design into a pattern, for construction, and for finishing.

Crystal Suspension
by Patricia Mattison, Wellsville, NY,
15" × 44", 2007

Brush Stroke by Emily Shuff
Klanberg, New York, NY,
33½" × 30¾", 2007

Photo by Katie Pasquini Masopust

Blendings by Katie Pasquini Masopust, 40" × 24", 2005

I made this fun little blending of colors for my daughter's wedding gift using a rainbow color scheme and vertical composition. The white bridal satin used for the background shows off the machine quilting stunningly. From the Barber collection.

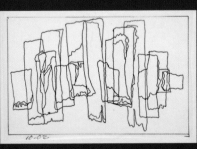

Acetate drawing for *Blendings* by Katie
Pasquini Masopust

Exploration for *Crystal
Suspension* by Patricia Mattison

Explorations for *Brush Stroke*
by Emily Shuff Klanberg

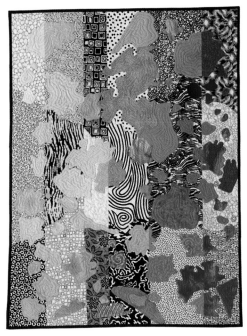

No Drop Cloth by
Robin Gausebeck,
Rockford, IL,
27½″ × 36″, 2007

Photo by Carolyn Wright

Splash I by Janet Ozard Root, Kendall, NY, 24″ × 41″, 2007

Vivace by Katie Pasquini Masopust, 48″ × 49″, 2006

I used the triad color scheme of red, yellow, and blue to create this piece. The original design was very static, so I played Jackson Pollock and "threw" paint on the surface with long fabric strips to represent the paint splatters. The swirling paint splatters energize the grid design. *Vivace* is a musical term meaning fast and lively.

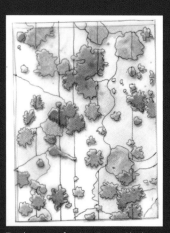

Exploration for *No Drop Cloth*
by Robin Gausebeck

Acetate drawing for *Vivace*
by Katie Pasquini Masopust

Exploration for *Splash I*
by Janet Ozard Root

exploring LINEAR REFLECTIONS

THIS EXPLORATION creates an abstract painting from an inspiration photo. The painting is done with watercolors, using straight-line brushstrokes of different widths to represent the elements in the image. The real objects in the inspirational photograph dictate the placement of the paint strokes. All the lines are parallel to the edges of the paper.

MATERIALS

Refer to pages 9–11 for tools and supplies.

- Watercolor paint
- ½″ flat paintbrush
- 8½″ × 11″ pad of watercolor paper
- Inspirational photographs
- Flat support to work on
- Matte acetate
- .01 Micron Pigma pen

INSTRUCTIONS

Create the Design

1. Collect photographs to use for inspiration.

2. Pick a color scheme from pages 14–17 and prepare the paint as described on page 54.

3. Create 3 different paintings from 1 image as described below.

Dry Painting

Use dry paper for the first painting. Using the landscape photo as an example, apply vertical and horizontal paint strokes parallel to the edges of the paper to designate the different areas (land, sky, and so on).

1. Determine where the lightest lights are and leave those areas as white paper.

2. Apply paint to the darkest areas—the shadows and the darkest of the foliage. Let the paint dry.

3. Apply paint to the medium and light areas.

4. Let each application dry before adding the next layer. Vary the width of the lines by occasionally using the side of the flat brush.

Inspirational landscape photo

Dry-paper watercolor painting using triad color scheme of red, yellow, and blue; paint dried between each application of color

Semidry Painting

Repeat the preceeding process, again starting with dry paper, but do not wait for the paint to dry completely before adding the next layer of colors. This will cause some blending of the overlapping colors.

Start with dry watercolor paper; add additional layers while paint is still damp.

Wet-on-Wet Painting

Repeat the process one last time on slightly dampened paper. Determine how long to wait before adding another layer of paint by deciding how much you want the colors to bleed into one another. The wetter the paint and paper, the more the additional colors will bleed.

Paint applied to wet paper without waiting between colors

Analyze the Designs

Analyze the paintings by answering the questions on page 20. Is there a good composition using the whole painting? If not, take the L-shaped cropping tool, and move it around the piece until you find the heart—an intriguing design. If you aren't satisfied, make more of these little studies, and analyze them.

Create the Quilt

Choose the strongest design and create a line drawing on acetate with the outline traced as a frame. Transform the design into an art quilt by following the instructions on pages 71–79 for turning a design into a pattern, for construction, and for finishing.

Photo by Carolyn Wright

Arpeggio by Katie Pasquini Masopust, 49″ × 62″, 2005

I used the triad color scheme of red, yellow, and blue to create this vertical composition. *Arpeggio* is a musical term describing a chord whose notes are performed in succession and not simultaneously.

Using the Cropping Tool

Rarely is my whole painting worthy of making into an art quilt. Using the cropping tool allows me to tighten up the composition and use only the part that makes a strong statement. This also takes the pressure off while painting. I don't worry if part of the painting isn't looking good. I know that when I am finished, I will use the cropping tool to find the very best part of the painting, the heart, to make into a quilt.

Second painting was strongest and was cropped to show intense play of lights and darks, cool and warm colors.

The Passage of Time by Kathy Downie, Richmond IL, 34″ × 25″, 2007

Somewhere by Joanne Pinckney, Gales Ferry, CT, 25″ × 40″, 2007

Exploration for *Somewhere* by Joanne Pinckney

Inspiration and exploration for *The Passage of Time* by Kathy Downie

exploring PALETTE KNIFE PAINTING

I N THIS exploration, a palette knife will be used to apply the paint. The palette knife creates a different mark than the paintbrush makes. Using a palette knife is like smoothing frosting on a cake. The acrylic paint will blend into beautiful lines of color when you are working wet paint on top of wet paint; or you can wait for the paint to dry before putting on a second layer, and hills and valleys of color will be created.

MATERIALS

Refer to pages 9–11 for tools and supplies.

- Canvas prepared with gesso
- Palette knives in different sizes
- Acrylic paints
- Light molding paste
- Masking tape
- Board support
- Matte acetate
- .01 Micron Pigma pen

INSTRUCTIONS

Create the Painting

1. Plan a color scheme you would like to work with, and select the appropriate colors of acrylic paints. Mix the selected colors with light molding paste to create the colors and values you desire. Light molding paste will thicken the paint so it can be scooped up and spread on the gessoed canvas with a palette knife.

2. Use masking tape to attach the gessoed canvas on all sides to a board support.

3. Scoop up the colored molding paste, and apply the paint to the surface. Have a plan for the marks of color—for example, vertical, horizontal, curved, grid, or some other scheme.

Triad color scheme in intense colors in medium value range

Triad color scheme in muted colors in medium value range

Triad color scheme in intense hues on black

Selecting a Color Scheme

Sometimes I am unsure what colors or even what values I want to use, so I make samples to try out possibilities. Here are two small pieces (12″ × 12″) in the triad color scheme of red, yellow, and blue. One is in a light to medium value range, and the other uses a full value range. I decided to use the light to medium value range because it is clean and joyful.

Little quilt in medium to dark value range

Little quilt in light to medium value range

Photo by Katie Pasquini Masopust

Analyze the Design

Analyze the painting for composition and interest by using the list of questions on page 20. If the entire painting is overwhelming, use the cropping tool to find the heart of the image within the painting.

Create the Quilt

Draw all the value changes, the blending of paint, and the color changes on matte acetate with a .01 Micron Pigma pen. Outline the finished design to frame it. Make this design into a quilt by following the instructions on pages 71–79 for turning a design into a pattern, for construction, and for finishing.

Use selected painting to create design on acetate.

Andante by Katie Pasquini Masopust, 45″ × 47″, 2007

The palette knife painting was the inspiration for *Andante*, a grid composition. I lightened the background strokes so that the pure colors appear to float off the surface. *Andante* is a musical term that means slowly, and this piece seems very peaceful and slow moving.

exploring
THE FREEZE FRAME

INSPIRATION IS everywhere. Can a scene found in nature or around the house, photographed from a unique angle, be the start of something marvelously abstract? In this exploration, challenge yourself to think differently about what you see. Use photographs of distinctive objects or images of moving elements to create freeze-frame designs.

MATERIALS

Refer to pages 9–11 for tools and supplies.

- Camera
- An inquisitive mind
- Matte acetate
- .01 Micron Pigma pen

INSTRUCTIONS

Find the Inspiration

1. Look around your environment, both indoors and outdoors. Search for interesting shapes and lines; notice how they are arranged. Inspiration can be provided by close-ups of leaves and rocks, cracks in the mud at the river's edge, running water, frozen water crystals, fire, arrangements of glasses, junk in a junk drawer—the list goes on and on.

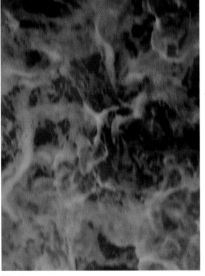

Water

Cracked mud

Fire

Photos by Katie Pasquini Masopust

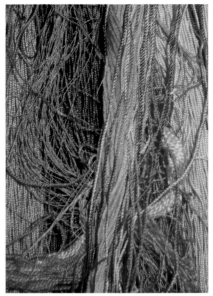

Photos by Katie Pasquini Masopust

Threads

Crystals

Ice

2. Take multiple pictures of your chosen subject. Compose the photos in a way that no one else would think to do. Photograph outside when there is a good contrast of light and dark, when the sun is rising or just about to set. Indoors, see what happens if you use a spotlight, or a flashlight, or a candle, or low light.

Analyze the Photos

Develop the film or download the digital images to your computer, and look for strong, interesting, and unique compositions. See if you need to use the cropping tool (page 9) to make the composition even tighter.

Create the Quilt

Draw your chosen design on matte acetate with a .01 Micron Pigma pen. Outline the design to make a frame. Make the design into a quilt by following the instructions on pages 71–79 for turning a design into a pattern, for construction, and for finishing.

Close-up of drinking glasses

Glass by Katie Pasquini Masopust, 45″ × 45″, 2007

I used a rainbow color scheme on gray with a circular composition. A close-up photograph of an assortment of drinking glasses was used as the inspiration.

Deconstructed by Kristina Cockerill, Oak Park, IL,
26″ × 38″, 2007

Photo by Carolyn Wright

Fire Dragon by Katie Pasquini Masopust, 23½″ × 35″, 2005

I selected the color scheme of analogous plus complement—red, orange, and yellow, with the complementary accent of blue-green in this asymmetric composition. I was delighted by my husband's comment that he noticed a dragon sitting in the flames. My brother-in-law, Jim, is a firefighter, and when he saw the quilt he told me a story of how firefighters see dragons in the flames when fighting big forest fires. The dragons can't be captured on film, but the firefighters have all seen them. So this is Jim's quilt. From the Robertson collection.

Exploration for *Deconstructed*
by Kristina Cockerill

Inspirational photo for *Fire Dragon*
by Katie Pasquini Masopust

from design TO PATTERN

YOU HAVE analyzed several designs and made improvements in them, and now it is time to create a pattern that will enable you to successfully make the quilt.

MATERIALS

- White paper
- Proportion scale
- Masking tape
- Poster board
- Spray adhesive
- Matte acetate with drawn design
- .01 Micron Pigma pen

INSTRUCTIONS

Plan the Colors

1. Choose the design you want to make into a quilt, and make sure you have a clean acetate drawing (created earlier in one of the exploration sections).

2. If you haven't already planned the colors, use graphite paper to transfer the design to watercolor paper, and make at least 3 different paintings with the possible color schemes you want to use (as described on pages 14–17). Choose the color scheme that feels right.

Three paintings for *Rainbow Lilies*

Enlarging Your Design

Using a proportional scale is an easy way to figure out what percentage to enlarge a drawing. There are two wheels on the proportional scale. The small wheel relates to the size of the small drawing. The large wheel relates to the size of the large quilt. The tool makes it easy. Just follow these steps:

1. Measure one side of the drawing. Let's say it is 8″. Find 8″ on the small wheel and hold it with your finger.

2. How long do you want that side of your quilt to be? Let's say you want it to be 35″. Roll the small wheel around until the 8″ mark is below the 35″ mark on the large wheel.

3. The wheel is set. Look into the window on the small wheel where it says, "percentage of original size." The arrow points to 440%. That is the percentage of enlargement. Ask the copy shop to set the copier to 440% to get the proper size.

4. You can also check to see what the other dimension of your quilt will be. Measure the other dimension of the drawing. Let's say the drawing is 8″ × 12″. Without moving the wheel, find 12″ on the small wheel and look to see what the measurement is on the large wheel. At 440%, the other dimension of your quilt will be 53″. If you enlarge your 8″ × 12″ drawing by 440%, your quilt will be 35″ × 53″.

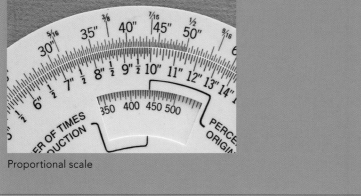

Proportional scale

Enlarge the Design

1. Cut the acetate ½″ larger than the drawn frame on the final matte acetate drawing. Tape a piece of white paper to the back of the acetate drawing. The white paper ensures that none of the shadows and lines from the copy machine will be picked up when the design is copied.

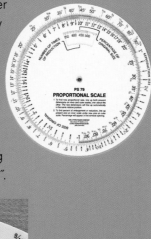

Prepare acetate for enlarging.

2. Decide what size you want the quilt to be. There are many reasons to choose a particular size. Is there a spot on your wall that you want the quilt to fit? Is there a size requirement for a show you would like to enter? If your design contains many small shapes, you may need to make a large quilt in order to be successful, as larger pieces are much easier to work with. Once you have determined the dimensions of the quilt, use a proportional scale to calculate the percentage the design will need to be enlarged.

If you don't have access to a proportional scale, you can figure the percentage of enlargement mathematically by dividing the size you want the quilt to be by the size of the drawing and then multiplying that number by 100.

3. Take the acetate line drawing, taped to a piece of clean white paper, to a copy shop, and have 3 enlarged copies made. Most larger copy shops have machines that can make copies up to 36″ wide. If your design will be larger than 36″, it will be enlarged in 36″-wide strips that can be taped together (on the back) to create the whole.

Copy #1

One of the enlarged copies will be used to create templates for the appliqué pieces. The following is the process:

1. Tape together poster board to create a piece that is the same size or larger than the copy. Tape the full length of the joint. Leave the taped side up.

2. Use spray adhesive to adhere the copy to the poster board. The tape is now on the inside, between the poster board and the pattern. (This will be important later if you use an iron to turn the edges. The iron won't touch the tape because it is between the poster board and the pattern.)

3. Cut out the shapes in the design to use as templates for cutting and turning the fabrics.

Copy #2

The second enlarged copy will be used as a map for the placement of the pieces as they are cut out.

Staple or pin this copy to your design wall. The design wall should be made of something that will be easy to pin or staple to, such as cork or Celotex (sometimes known as builder's board).

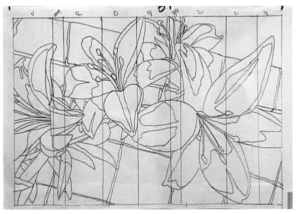

Secure placement map on design wall.

Copy #3

The third enlarged copy has multiple uses. One is for tracing the pattern onto stabilizer for appliqué (discussed in the following chapter). It also serves as a fail-safe in case you lose templates and need to make more, or if you need to look at something to see where your pieces go. This process is like putting together a jigsaw puzzle. Consider the third copy the puzzle box top that you refer to during construction.

Select Fabrics

Sort your fabrics into the seven value steps as explained on page 18. Arrange the fabrics so you can see all the colors and values.

You now have the patterns, guides, and fabrics you need to begin the quilt.

construction

YOU HAVE your pattern, and are ready to determine the best way to construct the quilt. If your pattern is based on one of the explorations using shape or line, the quilt can be constructed with machine piecing. If your pattern is based on one of the explorations using photographs or paintings, the construction can be done with my invisible-stitch appliqué technique.

MATERIALS

- Pattern
- Paper scissors
- Fabric scissors
- Fabric-marking pencils (I use Prismacolor colored pencils.)
- Quilting pins
- Glue stick

- Stabilizer forappliqué (I recommend Sulky Totally Stable.)
- Spray starch
- Stiletto
- Sewing machine with straight sewing foot and darning foot

- Thread for piecing and quilting
- Monofilament thread
- Optional: basting spray or safety pins for basting

INSTRUCTIONS

Cut Out the Fabrics

1. Place the fabric wrong side up, and place the pattern template wrong side up on top of it. Draw around the template with a fabric-marking pencil.

Place template upside down on fabric.

2. Cut the fabric ¼″ beyond the drawn line.

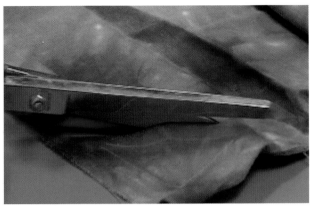

Cut ¼″ larger than drawn line.

3. Pin or staple the template and the fabric to the placement map on the design wall.

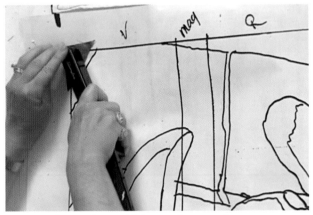

Pin or staple template and fabric to design wall.

4. Cut out all your pieces and pin or staple them to the design wall.

Assemble the Quilt Top

Checking Fabric Choices

When all of your cut-out fabrics are pinned to the wall, make sure all the fabric choices are right before you begin to sew. Look through a reducing glass or the wrong end of a pair of binoculars so you can see what the whole quilt will look like when it is sewn together. If there are fabrics that aren't working because they either demand too much attention, are not strong enough to show off a section, or are the wrong value, change them now. This is easy to do because the template is pinned in place behind the fabric. Remove the pieces that aren't working, and use the template to cut new pieces of fabric.

Machine Piecing

If your pieces are appropriate for machine piecing, follow these steps.

1. Select 2 adjoining pieces, and place them right sides together.

2. Pin the ends to align them. Depending on the length of the seam, you may need to put 1 or 2 pins between the 2 outside pins. Use the drawn lines to make sure the pieces are properly aligned.

3. Sew on the drawn line.

4. Press the seams open to create a smooth line.

5. Continue sewing the pieces together until the quilt top is complete.

Appliqué

If your pieces are appropriate for appliqué, follow these steps.

1. Use the third enlarged pattern copy to trace the design onto stabilizer, which will be used as the foundation for appliqué. I use Sulky Totally Stable, a heat-sensitive iron-on tear-away stabilizer. Draw the lines of the design on the shiny side of the stabilizer with a ballpoint pen. If the design is larger than the stabilizer, fasten several sheets of stabilizer together with small pieces of adhesive tape on the back.

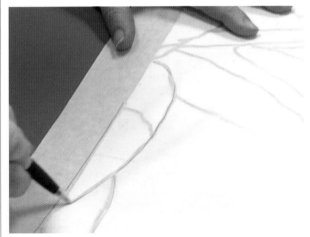

Draw design onto stabilizer.

2. Decide which piece to start with, and remove the appropriate fabric and pattern template from the wall. Use the pattern map to determine which edges of the fabric will lie on top of the adjoining pieces. These top edges will need to be turned.

3. Spray the fabric with spray starch.

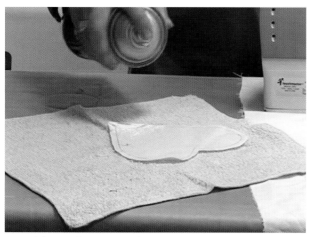

Spray fabric with spray starch.

4. Place the front side of the pattern template in place on the wrong side of the fabric. Turn the edge of the fabric over the template, and iron it in place with the aid of a stiletto. Make sure the spray starch is dry before you remove the template. Press the fabric piece once more to ensure that the edges are flat.

Turn edges of fabric over template for appliqué.

5. Place the fabric piece in position on the stabilizer, using the drawn lines to guide placement. Attach the prepared piece to the stabilizer with the tip of the iron. The pieces that are on top will have turned edges, and the pieces that are underneath will be left flat.

Attach prepared piece to stabilizer.

6. When all the pieces for a section of the quilt are in place, turn the stabilizer over and press lightly from the back to ensure that all the pieces are attached to the stabilizer and will stay in place. If there are small pieces that do not stick to the stabilizer, glue them in place with a glue stick.

7. Stitch the fabric in place. For hand appliqué, use a blind stitch. For free-motion invisible machine appliqué, use monofilament thread and set the machine to a zigzag with a stitch width of 2. Stitch around all the edges of the pieces to make sure everything is securely attached.

8. Work in small sections, ironing the pieces to the stabilizer, then sewing them down. Continue this process until all the pieces are in place.

9. Remove the stabilizer when all the pieces have been sewn into place and your quilt top is complete.

Free-Motion Invisible Machine Appliqué

I don't drop the feed dogs (but I do use a darning foot) when I free-motion stitch. I like the extra tension or grip the feed dogs provide, making it easier for me to sew because the fabric doesn't slip as readily. Because the stitching is invisible, my main concern is that all the pieces are securely stitched; I don't worry too much about how each stitch looks. On some machines you do need to drop the feed dogs. If you have the option, experiment and see which works best for you.

Free-motion invisible machine appliqué

Baste

Cut backing fabric and batting 2″ larger all around than the quilt top. Make a quilt sandwich by placing the 3 layers (backing, batting, and quilt top) in position on a flat surface. Basting holds together the 3 layers so they can be quilted. The basting can be done by hand with large running stitches, with safety pins, or with a spray-baste adhesive.

Spray Basting
When using spray adhesives, work outside or in a very well-ventilated room.

1. Fold back half of the top layer of the quilt sandwich, and spray the batting with adhesive. Smooth out that half.

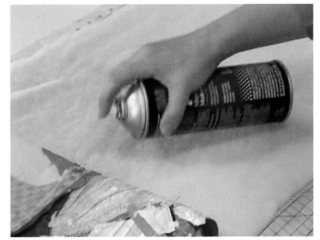

Spray baste half of quilt top.

2. Repeat with the other half.

3. Turn over the quilt sandwich and follow the same instructions for the backing.

4. Use an iron to press the whole quilt from the back to flatten the batting.

Quilt

Quilting not only holds the layers together; it is an opportunity to enhance your design.

Hand Quilting

For hand quilting, place the basted quilt sandwich in a hoop or a frame, and quilt the layers together with small running stitches. Draw the quilting design on the surface with a fabric-marking pencil, or quilt free-form.

Machine Quilting

You can machine quilt using any method you choose. I prefer free-motion quilting. I use the zigzag setting on my machine, with the stitch width set to 0. This 0 setting will stitch a straight stitch. When I want to create dimension, I adjust the width of the stitch while I am sewing to add a variety of satin-stitch lines where desired.

Sign your name in the lower right-hand corner while machine quilting. I usually just put my first name and the date the quilt was finished.

finishing

BLOCK THE QUILT

The finished piece must be square or true to the shape intended. The quilt should be blocked so it will lie flat.

1. Place the quilt on a flat surface.

2. Steam the entire surface with a steamer. This can be a professional steamer like the ones used to steam clothes in a dress shop, or it can be an iron that has a steam setting. Start in the center and work out in circles to the outside edge.

3. Let the quilt dry overnight before moving it.

SQUARE THE QUILT

Squaring means trimming the edges of the quilt so the corners are 90°, or true right angles. If your quilt is not meant to be a square or rectangle, trim as needed.

1. Move the blocked quilt to a large rotary cutting mat.

2. Use a T-square to line up the corners, and trim away anything outside the desired edge.

MAKE A SLEEVE

If your quilt is square or rectangular, a simple sleeve running along the top edge, which a rod can be put through, is the easiest way to display a quilt on a wall. If the quilt has irregular edges, rings can be attached so it can be hooked onto nails in the wall.

Follow these steps to make a hanging sleeve.

1. Cut a strip of fabric 9″ wide by the length of the top edge of the quilt.

2. Turn under the 2 short edges so they won't get caught in the binding on the sides of the quilt, and stitch.

3. Fold the sleeve in half, with the right side out, and pin the unturned edges of the sleeve to the top edge of the quilt, matching the raw edges. These edges will be stitched into the binding.

4. Hand stitch the folded edge to the back of the quilt.

Make fabric sleeve for hanging.

MAKE A LABEL

Use your inspiration photo or painting to create a label. If you are comfortable using a computer, there are many ways to print on fabric using an inkjet printer. The following is another way to create a label.

1. Place the inspiration onto a piece of white paper.

2. Write the quilt title, the size, the date it was completed, and your name, city, and state on the paper.

3. Transfer the image to white fabric using a photo transfer technique. You may have to reduce the image when transferring it to make the label a manageable size.

4. Pin the label to the lower right-hand side of the back of the quilt. The outer edges will be stitched into the binding. Hand stitch the remaining edges of the label.

Create fabric label.

BIND THE QUILT

Binding will finish the raw outside edge of the quilt.

1. Cut fabric on the bias in 1¾″-wide strips.

2. Sew these lengths end-to-end on the diagonal until the strip is long enough to go around the outside edge of the quilt, with some extra for turning corners.

3. Press the strip in half lengthwise, right side out. Machine sew the raw edges to the front of the quilt, right sides together, stitching through the sleeve and the label.

4. Roll the folded edge of the binding to the back of the quilt, and blind stitch in place by hand.

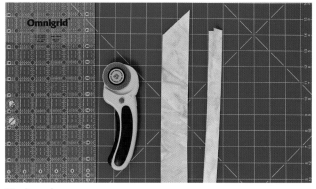

Binding

DOCUMENT THE QUILT

The final stage of the process is to document all that you have done. This is especially important if you plan to enter your art quilt into a competition.

1. Have the finished quilt photographed by a professional. You may wish to have slides, a 4″ × 5″ transparency, and digital images. Have digital images made in .jpg versions for emailing, and .tifs for reproduction in print.

2. Keep a file of your work that includes the date you finished the quilt, the size, and the title. Keep notes on the techniques used and your inspiration. This will make it easy to fill out forms and answer requests when entering your work in shows or for publication.

You are done! Hang your quilt on the wall and enjoy your accomplishment.

Congratulations!

About the Author

Fiber artist Katie Pasquini Masopust has traveled throughout the United States and to Canada, New Zealand, Australia, Japan, Belgium, Switzerland, Norway, Denmark, and England teaching contemporary quilt design. She has changed her style several times over the years. After starting with traditional works, she next turned to creating mandalas, followed by dimensional quilts. She then moved on to landscapes, fracturing them and adding transparencies and color washes. Her most recent work is based on her acrylic paintings. She feels that she has come full circle, returning to her beginnings as a painter, but painting now with fabric. Katie teaches in a relaxed but energizing style, passing her extensive knowledge of design and the art quilt on to her students.

Katie has won many awards throughout her career, including receiving the Silver Star Award at the International Quilt Festival in Houston.

Visit Katie's website at www.katiepm.com.

ALSO BY KATIE PASQUINI MASOPUST

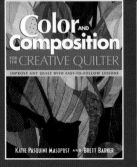

Index

For a list of other fine books from C&T Publishing, ask for a free catalog:

C&T Publishing, Inc.
P.O. Box 1456
Lafayette, CA 94549
(800) 284-1111
Email: ctinfo@ctpub.com
www.ctpub.com

C&T Publishing's professional photography services are now available to the public. Visit us at **www.ctmediaservices.com**.

For quilting supplies:
Cotton Patch
1025 Brown Ave.
Lafayette, CA 94549
(800) 835-4418 or
(925) 283-7883
Email: CottonPa@aol.com
www.quiltusa.com

Note: Fabrics used in the quilts shown may not be currently available, as fabric manufacturers keep most fabrics in print for only a short time.